Dark Zones

Exploring Caves

By Julie Haydon

NELSON
CENGAGE Learning

Australia • Brazil • Japan • Korea • Mexico • Singapore • Spain • United Kingdom • United States

NELSON
CENGAGE Learning

Dark Zones

Text: Julie Haydon
Design: Karen Mayo
Editor: Barb Whiter
Illustrations: Alan Laver

Acknowledgements
The author would like to thank Ken Grimes for kindly
agreeing to review the manuscript, and Dale Appleton, Ken
Boland, Paul Brooker, Belinda Cardinal, Alex Kariko,
Norman Poulter (OAM), Roy Swain, Roger Taylor and the
Victorian Speleological Associan for their generous
assistance.
Photographs by Stephen Alvarez/Sport. The Library, pp. 22
(bottom), 31 (top right); Australian Picture Library/Corbis,
p. 31 (bottom); Australian Picture Library/Sharpshooters
Premium Stock Photography, p. 12 (left); Andy
Belcher/Auscape, p. 18 and front cover (bottom left); Hans
& Judy Beste/Lochman Transparencies, pp. 13 (bottom), 17
(bottom); Nicholas Birks/Auscape, p. 15 and front cover
(bottom right); Ken Boland, pp. 5, 9 (top right), 20 (centre),
21 (bottom), 22 (centre), 23 (top), 25, front cover (top) and
back cover; Brett Dennis/Lochman Transparencies, p. 9
(bottom); Jean-Paul Ferrero /Auscape, pp. 12 (top), 14, 16, 31
(top left); Didier Givois/Sport. The Library, p. 21 (top); K. G.
Grimes, pp. 11, 20 (top), 22 (top), 23 (bottom); Greg Harold
/Auscape, p. 12 (bottom far right); Jiri Lochman/Lochman
Transparencies, pp. 8, 12 (centre top, bottom centre, and
right centre above and below), 13 (top centre), 17 (top,
second from top, and centre), 28; Steve
Lovegrove/Tasmanian Photo Library, pp. 6, 27 (top); Peter
Marsack/Lochman Transparencies, p. 17 (second from
bottom); Reg Morrison/Auscape, p. 10 (bottom); Geoff
Murray/Tasmanian Photo Library, pp. 2-3, 4, 32-3;
Michael/Nichols/Sport. The Library, p. 30; Norman Poulter,
pp. 1, 9 (top left), 10 (top), 13 (right), 20 (bottom), 26, 29;
Dennis Sarson/Lochman Transparencies, pp. 13 (top left),
and 17 (third from top and third from bottom); Ronald
Sheridan/Ancient Art & Architecture Collection, p. 27
(bottom); Mark Spencer/Auscape, p. 24.

Text © 2001 Julie Haydon
Illustrations © 2001 Cengage Learning Australia Pty Limited

For product information and technology assistance,
in Australia call 1300 790 853;
in New Zealand call 0508 635 766

For permission to use material from this text or product,
please email aust.permissions@cengage.com

ISBN 978 1 86 961489 8
ISBN 978 1 86 961483 6 (set)

Cengage Learning Australia
Level 7, 80 Dorcas Street
South Melbourne, Victoria Australia 3205

Cengage Learning New Zealand
Unit 4B Rosedale Office Park
331 Rosedale Road, Albany, North Shore NZ 0632

For learning solutions, visit cengage.com.au

Printed in China by 1010 Printing International Ltd
10 11 12 13 12 11 10

Contents

Introduction

Imagine what it's like to explore a cave. It is so exciting to be under the earth's surface. You move from what is known as the *twilight zone* through to the *dark zone* of the cave. There is no sunlight here, no green plants, no birds. The only light is from your flashlight or the light on the front of your helmet. When you speak, your voice echoes in the cave's chamber. And all the while, you can hear the constant drip, drip, drip of water.

In the small pool of light created by the flashlight, you see a *stalagmite*. It is as tall as you are and is a rich, glowing orange. Above it is a *stalactite*. Perhaps, in a few thousand years, they will join up and form a *column*.

Most people think that caves are dark and scary places, cold and lifeless like a tomb, but caves do contain life — you just have to look closely!

Exploring caves can be a dangerous activity. Never enter a cave alone or without the proper training or equipment.

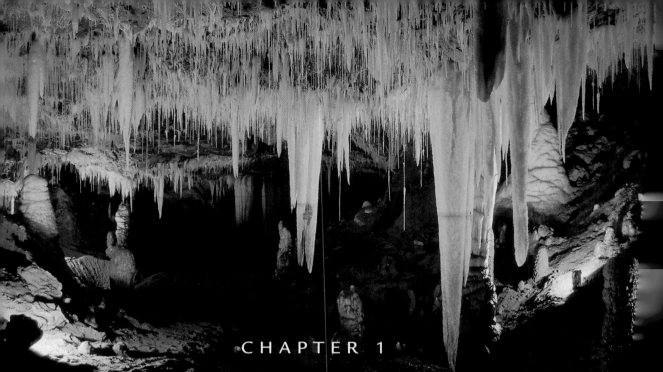

What Is a Cave?

A cave is a natural cavity beneath the earth's surface. Some caves are small. Others, like the world's largest cave system, Mammoth Cave in Kentucky, USA, are enormous. Mammoth Cave is over 560 kilometres long! The only way to explore and map a cave is to walk, crawl, wade, climb (and sometimes scuba dive) through its interior.

But it would be wrong to picture Mammoth Cave as just one long tunnel. It has winding passages that spread over numerous levels and the system also contains rivers with names like Echo and Styx. Water is common in many caves. It creates most of the spectacular rock formations which are found inside caves.

CAVE QUIZ

What is the difference between a cave and a mine?

Answer: A cave is made by nature, a mine is made by people.

How Are Caves Formed?

Limestone and Water

Imagine you are standing in a huge cave. It is very quiet. The light from your flashlight shows the roof of the cave chamber far above. Stunning rock formations hang from the roof and also thrust upwards from the ground. Ahead is an inky river. It moves almost silently. In its waters are strange, pale creatures. They are blind.

You step forward and touch the cave wall. This huge cave is made of *limestone*. The world's largest and deepest caves are formed from limestone and water. It is hard to believe that this cave did not always exist, and in its place was solid limestone. You wonder how this cave was created. The illustrations on the next page show how a cave forms in limestone rock.

CAVE QUIZ

What is limestone made of?

Answer: Limestone is composed of calcium carbonate, made from the compacted remains of many marine animals. Some are microscopic in size, including corals and algae.

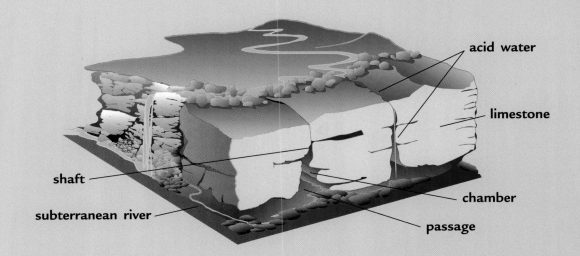

acid water

limestone

shaft

chamber

subterranean river

passage

1. When rain falls, it absorbs a gas called *carbon dioxide* from the air and the soil. This gas turns the water into a weak acid, which seeps into cracks in the limestone rock beneath the soil.

2. The acid water begins to dissolve the rock. Holes form. More acid water seeps into the holes, enlarging them. Over many thousands of years, these holes become the chambers, passages and shafts of a cave.

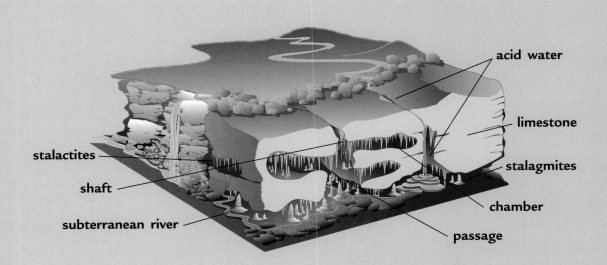

acid water

limestone

stalactites

stalagmites

shaft

chamber

subterranean river

passage

3. Rain continues to fall, seeping down through the cave. *Subterranean* rivers form. The rivers *erode* more limestone and the water travels further down through the rock.

CHAPTER 2

Cave Formations

Nature can create beautiful things — just look at the cave formations in the photograph above. These formations come in varied colours such as white, tan and red. They can be shaped like icicles, cones, flowers, crazy twists and curls, and even curtains. Cave formations are called *speleothems* and they help transform the dark interior of a limestone cave into an exciting wonderland for cavers.

Speleothems, like the caves themselves, are formed by water. The part of the limestone that is dissolved and carried away by acid water is called *calcium carbonate*. As the water travels through the cave, it leaves behind a mineral called *calcite*. Most speleothems are made from calcite. The best known speleothems are stalactites, which grow down from the ceiling, and

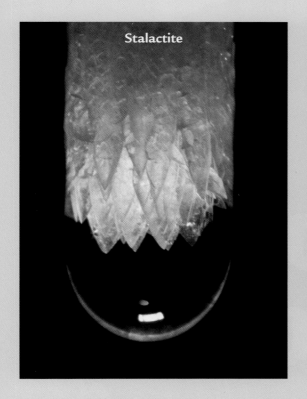

Stalactite

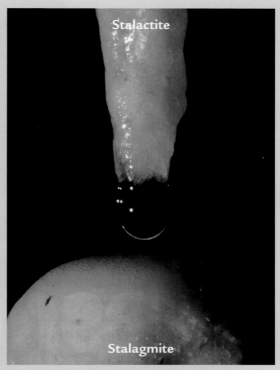

Stalactite

Stalagmite

Stalactites

As acid water seeps through limestone rock and onto the ceiling of a cave, calcite is deposited on the cave ceiling in a little ring. Slowly, a hollow tube, or 'straw', forms. If the straw becomes blocked, a thicker stalactite forms.

Stalagmites

When drops of water fall to the ground (often from the end of a stalactite), the calcite builds up and a stalagmite forms on the floor of the cave.

CAVE QUIZ

What determines the colour of a speleothem?

Answer: Its mineral content. Calcite is white, but when it combines with other minerals, brightly coloured speleothems can occur.

9

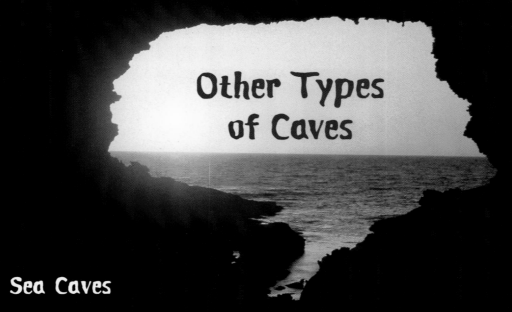

Other Types of Caves

Sea Caves

Not all caves are formed in limestone. Sea caves are formed by the pounding of waves against seaside cliffs. They are short-lived caves, as they are continually being eroded by the salt water, and the sand and rocks that the waves contain. If a sea cave's roof collapses, a blowhole may form. Marine animals, such as seals, often use sea caves as resting places.

These caves can be dangerous to explore. The water level in a sea cave can alter quickly with the changing of the tide.

Lava Caves

When a volcano erupts, hot molten rock, known as lava, often flows from it. The outside of the lava flow is exposed to the air and ground, and cools first, and a hard shell may form. The molten lava inside continues to flow, draining away. The hollow tube that is left behind is a lava cave.

Glacier Caves

Glaciers are rivers of ice that move slowly down mountains. When a glacier starts to melt, the water sometimes runs under the ice or through cracks in the ice. A cave with walls and a roof of ice is formed.

Glacier caves are the most dangerous above-water caves to explore because they are slippery, and can collapse without warning.

CAVE QUIZ

What name do we give a coastline that is being eroded by sea water?

Answer: A retreating coastline.

CHAPTER 3
Cave Inhabitants

What creatures live in caves? First you need to remember a cave has two zones. Imagine you are entering a cave. You step into the twilight zone. It does not feel too strange as there is some sunlight here, plus ferns and mosses, and you can still see and hear birds and other animals from outside the cave.

owls

Trogloxenes: Cave Visitors

Trogloxenes may sleep or spend each winter in caves, but they live only part of their lives in caves.

snakes

possums

bears

flies

frogs

lizards

Walk further in. Turn on your helmet light or flashlight, because you are entering the dark zone, a world of permanent darkness. Here there is no difference between day and night. It is cold and damp, and it smells musty. You might wonder how a cave can support any life. Certainly humans could not live for long in the dark zone, but there are many creatures for which the dark zone of a cave is home.

CAVE QUIZ

Why are the inhabitants of a cave's dark zone usually blind and colourless?

Answer: In the dark, there is no need for sight, or for body colour to provide camouflage or protection from the sun.

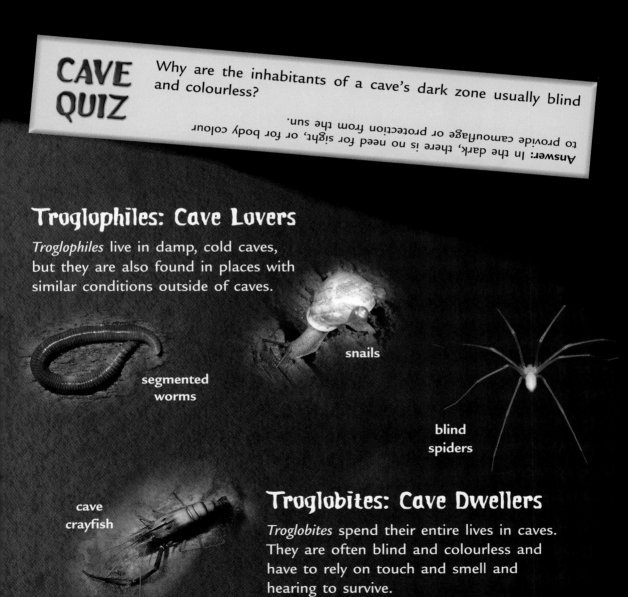

Troglophiles: Cave Lovers

Troglophiles live in damp, cold caves, but they are also found in places with similar conditions outside of caves.

segmented worms

snails

blind spiders

cave crayfish

Troglobites: Cave Dwellers

Troglobites spend their entire lives in caves. They are often blind and colourless and have to rely on touch and smell and hearing to survive.

13

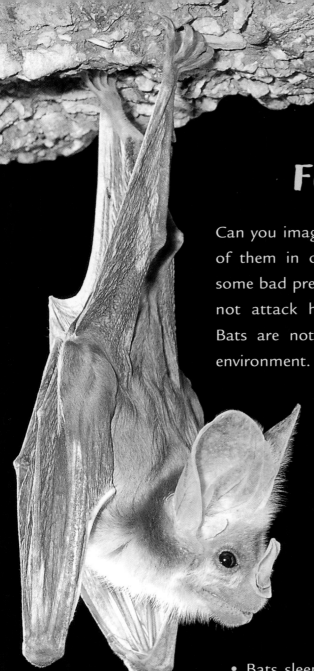

Fascinating Bats

Can you imagine a cave full of bats? Tens of thousands of them in one cave! Over the years, bats have had some bad press, especially in horror movies, but bats do not attack humans or get caught in people's hair. Bats are not vicious. In fact, bats are good for the environment. Most cave-dwelling bats are *insectivores*. They eat insects that would otherwise destroy farmers' crops.

Bat Facts:

- Bats are the only mammals that can fly.

- Bats are nocturnal, so they are active at night and rest during the day.

- Bats can live in caves, trees, deserts, even in house attics.

- Bats sleep hanging upside down and often in huge clusters to keep warm.

- Bats have babies called pups.

- Cave-dwelling bats often hibernate or migrate during winter. If you see a hibernating bat, leave it alone. If you wake it, it will use precious energy that it needs to survive the winter.

How do bats get around in caves and at night? They use *echolocation*. Most bats can actually see very well, but eyesight is of little use in the dark, so many bats 'see' by listening to echoes.

A bat emits high-pitched sounds which bounce off objects around it. The bat listens to the echoes and is able to judge how far away an object is, its size and whether it is moving.

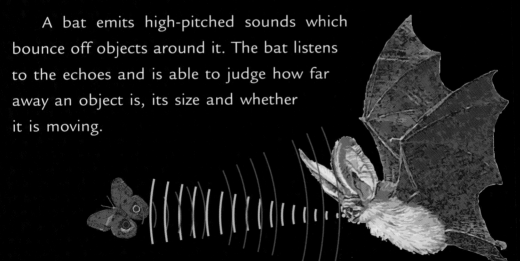

CAVE QUIZ

Bats are nocturnal animals.
What do we call animals that are active during the day?

Answer: Diurnal animals.
An easy way to remember is Night = Nocturnal, Day = Diurnal.

CHAPTER 4
Food Chain

Have you begun to wonder about the food chain inside a cave? If a bat died and fell to the floor of the cave, do you think it would become food for other, smaller cave creatures?

The food chain inside a cave may not be easy to detect at first, but if you look carefully, you will see that a cave does offer feeding opportunities. There is no sunlight in a cave's dark zone, so no green plants can grow. A cave is a barren place. But because a cave is not cut off from the world outside, food can walk, slither or fly in, be carried in by bats and other creatures, or be brought in by a cave's rivers and streams.

CAVE QUIZ

Which cave inhabitants create their own light to attract food?

Answer: Australian and New Zealand glow-worms. A sticky thread hangs beneath each glow-worm's light. When an insect flies towards the light, it becomes caught on the thread and is eaten by the glow-worm.

Feeding Opportunities

A cave floor is covered in bat and cricket droppings (known as *guano*), insect eggs, dead insects, and leaves and plants that have been washed in by rain and floods.

The cycle of feeding continues.

A cave cricket also returns from feeding outside the cave. It adds its droppings to the rich pile of guano on the cave floor.

Meanwhile, a bat returns from its nightly feeding. Its stomach is full of insects found outside the cave. The bat's droppings fall to the ground.

Young blind crayfish are eaten by cave fish and salamanders.

Salamander *larvae* eat the amphipods and isopods.

Amphipods and isopods also eat dead leaves.

The copepods are eaten by *amphipods*, *isopods* and blind crayfish.

Snails and roundworms eat the guano.

Beetles and spiders eat the insect eggs and the dead insects.

Fungi and *bacteria* grow on the guano, the dead insects and the dead plants.

The fungi and bacteria are eaten by mites, *springtails* and crickets.

The mites, springtails, snails and roundworms are eaten by beetles and centipedes.

Some of the beetles and centipedes fall into the cave's stream and are eaten by salamanders, blind crayfish and cave fish.

Fungi in the stream is eaten by *copepods*.

CHAPTER 5
Caving

People who explore caves are called 'cavers'. The types of equipment cavers use include the following:

Clothing:

thick coveralls

a hard hat with chin strap and light

protective knee and elbow pads

strong boots with good tread

Contents of a Rucksack:

- a flashlight and batteries
- a spare flashlight and spare batteries
- a candle and matches in a waterproof container
- drinking water
- food in a waterproof container
- a first aid kit
- spare clothing and gloves (for long trips and cold caves)
- a space blanket
- a compass
- a map of the cave

Group Equipment:

(may vary depending on the type of cave)

- harnesses
- ropes
- caving ladder
- *carabiners*
- *descenders* and *ascenders*
- pulleys
- nylon tape
- whistles
- scuba diving equipment (if cave diving)

Danger! Danger!

Caving is a dangerous activity. That's why all cavers need to be prepared.

Let's pretend a group of experienced cavers has been underground for over two hours. There is an unexpected rock fall. Now their way back is blocked. They must turn around, wade through a cold river and wriggle through a narrow passage called a squeeze, before they can pick up the original trail. Luckily, their leader has a map.

Remember, this is all done in darkness, except for the small pool of light from each caver's helmet light or flashlight!

Sometimes, cavers fall down vertical shafts, called *pitches*. They can be hit by rockfalls, or be trapped when a passage suddenly floods. This is why cavers always explore in a group, with an experienced leader. Everyone must know what equipment to use and how to use it.

All cavers must follow the safety rules every time they go caving.

Safety Rules

- Never enter a cave alone.

- Always tell an adult where you will be and when you expect to return.

- Always have an experienced adult with you.

- Wear warm, suitable clothing.

- Never go into a cave when it is raining or might rain, as the cave might flood.

- Always carry a flashlight, spare batteries, candles and matches.

- Always wear a watch.

- Never run or jump in a cave.

- Never drink cave water.

- Never touch cave animals or plants.

- Take nothing from a cave and leave nothing behind.

- Never try any caving task beyond your abilities.

- Turn back if tired.

- Remember that the return trip usually takes longer.

CAVE QUIZ

Why should you carry your main light on your helmet?

Answer: To keep your hands free and to provide a source of light near your eyes.

CHAPTER 6
Caving Techniques

There are techniques you need to learn to become a caver and explore caves safely. Do not attempt any of these alone or without proper training and supervision — remember the safety rules you've just read!

Horizontal Techniques

You might begin by walking through a cave's twilight zone, but as the cave's passages become narrower and darker, you will soon be stooping and crawling (that's why you need knee pads) and squeezing your body through tight spots.

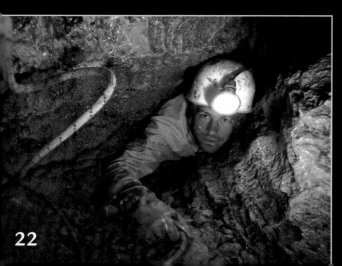

If you encounter shallow water, then you might have to wade through it, or cross it by climbing the walls above it without using ropes — this is known as traversing. If the passage is completely flooded, you will probably need scuba diving equipment to go any further.

Vertical Techniques

To go up or down a pitch, you will need a caving ladder and ropes or you might *abseil* down wearing a harness, and *prusik* up using the harness, ascenders and foot loops in the rope.

CAVE QUIZ

In what other sports do people abseil?

Answer: Mountaineering, canyoning and rock-climbing.

23

Cave Diving

Cave divers explore caves that are underwater. Cave diving is a specialised sport.

A cave diver must first learn how to scuba dive in a safe environment before attempting a cave dive. After all, in an underwater cave you can't come up to the surface if you run out of air.

Cave divers wear wetsuits and use scuba diving equipment, such as air tanks with valves and hoses, lights, flippers, masks and waterproof watches. The water in caves is often murky, so cave divers unroll lines as they explore so they can find their way out again.

Cave diving can be very dangerous.

CAVE QUIZ

What do you call a cave passage that is completely flooded?

Answer: A sump.

CHAPTER 7

Getting Started

If you want to try caving, here are a few hints:

1. Join a caving group. Most countries have speleological associations or societies and they will be able to give you the name of your local club.

2. Visit developed caves. These are caves that are open to the public and they usually have well-lit paths. Take guided tours.

3. Learn caving techniques, such as abseiling and ladder work, above ground. Many caving clubs practise in gymnasiums.

4. Visit Internet sites and read books on caving.

CAVE QUIZ

What is the name given to undeveloped caves that have no paths and no electric lights, and you often require permission to enter?

Answer: Wild caves.

CHAPTER 8

What Is a Speleologist?

A speleologist is a person who studies caves. Sometimes, speleologists will stay underground for days, with no light other than that which they have been able to carry in with them. A French scientist once lived in the dark zone of a cave for six months. He was helping an American government agency, NASA (National Aeronautics and Space Administration), study the effects of being alone in space.

Speleologists study:

1. how caves form
2. how cave animals live
3. underground rivers
4. archaeological remains

All caves 'breathe'. This speleologist is measuring the speed of the wind as it exits a cave.

Speleologists also survey caves and produce detailed maps. Sometimes speleologists will put dye in a cave river or stream, so they can see where the river or stream exits the cave.

CHAPTER 9
A Fragile Environment

When people break speleothems, damage fragile sections of a cave floor, or spray or scratch graffiti in a cave, they are destroying something which has taken nature hundreds or thousands of years to create.

People cave for different reasons — the thrill and challenge of exploring, the hope of discovering a new cave, to take photographs, or to look for cave paintings. Whatever the reason, a caver must always remember to 'cave softly'.

Caves are valuable and beautiful places. We must work to keep

To 'cave softly' means:

- Never forget that a cave is home to many creatures. If you damage any part of a cave, you may be putting creatures' lives at risk. Do not touch any cave fauna or flora for any reason.

- Always stay on the established paths in a cave and do not make any permanent marks on the cave walls, floor or ceiling.

- Do not litter or break off pieces of speleothems for souvenirs.

A speleologist lays a plastic cover on a pathway to protect a fragile cave floor.

CAVE QUIZ

Why must a caver avoid touching speleothems?

Answer: Because the speleothems may break, and the oil from human hands can damage them.

CHAPTER 10

Famous Caves

Some famous caves around the world have already been mentioned, like Mammoth Cave and Lascaux Cave, but here are a few more you may like to research and visit one day.

The Big Room in Carlsbad Caverns, New Mexico, can hold 14 football fields and is 25 storeys high.

CAVE QUIZ The Carlsbad Caverns in New Mexico were discovered in 1898, when a cowboy went to investigate what he thought was a black cloud of smoke rising from a hole in the ground at dusk. The hole was an entrance to the Caverns, but the cloud was not smoke. What was it?

Answer: Hundreds of thousands of bats leaving the Caverns to feed.

Glow-worms illuminate
New Zealand's
Waitomo Caves.

Mystery Falls,
in Chattanooga,
Tennessee, was once
used as a water source
for the township.
However the spectacular
91-metre underground
waterfall is no longer
open to the public.

Sarawak Cavern in
Malaysia is the world's
largest cave chamber.
It is 700 metres long,
430 metres wide
and approximately
100 metres high.

CAVE QUIZ

What is the deepest cave in the world?

Answer: Jean Bernard Cave in France at 1602 metres deep.

Glossary

abseil	to slide down using a rope and wearing a harness
amphipods	creatures such as freshwater shrimps
ascenders	metal clamping devices that will slide up a rope but not down
bacteria	organisms too small to be seen by humans
calcite	a mineral made of calcium carbonate
calcium carbonate	a white substance that makes up chalk and limestone
carbon dioxide	a colourless, odourless gas
carabiners	metal links for attaching to ropes
column	the formation that is created when a stalactite and stalagmite join up
copepods	tiny creatures that live in water
dark zone	the part of a cave that is constantly in darkness
descenders	metal friction devices attached to a rope, and used during abseiling to control the speed of descent
echolocation	a way of locating objects by detecting sounds
erode	to eat away at something
fungi	organisms, such as mushrooms, that live off dead or living animals and plants
guano	animal droppings that are an important part of the food chain in many caves
insectivores	animals that eat insects
isopods	creatures with seven pairs of legs, such as wood lice
larvae	the young of some insects
limestone	rock consisting mainly of calcium carbonate
pitches	vertical shafts in a cave
prusik	to move up a rope using a harness, ascenders and foot loops in the rope
speleothems	formations in caves usually made up of the mineral calcite
springtails	wingless insects that can leap into the air
stalactite	a speleothem that hangs from a cave's ceiling
stalagmite	a speleothem that grows upwards on a cave's floor
subterranean	underground
troglobites	creatures that spend their entire lives in caves
troglophiles	creatures that live in caves
trogloxenes	creatures that live only part of their lives in caves
twilight zone	the part of a cave that receives some sunlight

Further Reading

Eyewitness Visual Dictionaries, 1993, *The Visual Dictionary of the Earth*, Dorling Kindersley, London

Prior, Natalie Jane, 1996, *Caves, Graves and Catacombs*, Allen & Unwin, Sydney

Rigby, Susan, 1994, *Our Planet: Caves*, Troll Associates, Mahwah